GRACE CATALANO

**An Unauthorized
Biography**

BANTAM BOOKS

NEW YORK • TORONTO • LONDON • SYDNEY • AUCKLAND

RL 5, age 10 and up

JUST JASON

A Bantam Book / December 1991

The Starfire logo is a registered trademark of Bantam Books,
a division of Bantam Doubleday Dell Publishing Group, Inc.
Registered in U.S. Patent and Trademark Office and elsewhere.

ISBN 0-553-29816-X

Published simultaneously in the United States and Canada

Bantam Books are published by Bantam Books, a division of
Bantam Doubleday Dell Publishing Group, Inc. Its trademark,
consisting of the words "Bantam Books" and the portrayal of a
rooster, is Registered in U.S. Patent and Trademark Office and in
other countries. Marca Registrada. Bantam Books, 666 Fifth
Avenue, New York, New York 10103.

PRINTED IN THE UNITED STATES OF AMERICA

RAD   0 9 8 7 6 5 4 3 2 1

The author would like to thank: Sam Alan, Grace Palazzo, Ralph J. Miele, Mary Michaels, and Jane Burns.

Also, thanks to Beverly Horowitz and Diana Ajjan at Bantam Books.

And all my love to Rosemarie, Salvatore, and Joseph, who continue to support me!

CONTENTS

Introduction   ix

1 In the Beginning   1

2 Child Star   8

3 The Teenage Rebel   13

4 Back to Acting   22

5 Next Stop—Hollywood   31

6 Racing to Stardom   41

7 The Hit Show—*Beverly Hills,
90210*   48

8 On the Set with the 90210 Gang   66

9 Jason's Romantic Side   78

10 The Secret of His Success   85

11 "This Is Who I Really Am!"   93

12 New Directions   101

Jason's Checklist Fact File   106

Juicy Jason Secrets   109

Hey, Jay, What Do You Say?   112

INTRODUCTION

When Jason Priestley is asked to comment on his enormous popularity, his response is modest for someone so famous. "I don't know, it's all so new to me," he says softly. "I wasn't on the covers of magazines yesterday."

Today, he's the hottest young actor on the hottest TV show, *Beverly Hills, 90210*. The hour-long drama has become a lodestone to teenagers across the country, and one of the main reasons for all the pandemonium is Jason Priestley. The versatile superstar, who plays clean-cut good guy Brandon Walsh, is intense, sensitive, and gorgeous. His twinkling blue-green-gray eyes send sparks from the screen, and his candid, refreshing personality may be the reason for his universal appeal. Jason Priestley seems to be doing everything just right.

In February 1991, 90210 slowly began to climb the ratings chart, and at the same time, Jason began the climb up to the teen-idol throne. In just two months, he reached it, and since then his easygoing, tough-but-tender manner and devilish grin have charmed his many fans.

He's being hailed as one of the most exciting young stars in the business. *People* magazine called him "TV's Coolest Kid" and promptly named him one of "the 50 Most Beautiful People in the World." His mail increases every day (he now receives approximately 1,500 letters a week) and he has fans all over the world, including England, where 90210 is the number one TV show.

It's a lot to handle, but Jason is managing fame well, even though his rapid success continues to surprise him. He hopes to remain the same person he was before stardom hit, but can he? Can things ever be the same again? Can he stay unaffected by his success?

Jason maintains an honest attitude; he

isn't the kind of guy to let fame go to his head. He is just like the guy who lives up the block. With all the success and adulation that have come his way, Jason has worked hard not to let it alter his life-style. The trappings of Hollywood mean little to him.

"I don't get up in the morning and look in the mirror and say, 'Hey, Jay baby, lookin' good today,' " explains the incredibly down-to-earth star. "I get up and say, 'Where's the Visine?' "

Trying to maintain his "ordinary guy" appearance, Jason prefers wearing jeans and a T-shirt to expensive clothes. He would rather play hockey or basketball than go to a glitzy Hollywood party. In fact, one of his favorite pastimes is playing hockey (position—center) with the Celebrity All-Stars Team, which includes Michael J. Fox and *MacGyver*'s Richard Dean Anderson.

Jason is most concerned with the way he comes across in interviews. "My fear is sounding arrogant," he explains. "I'm always monitoring myself to make sure I don't become pretentious or pompous."

Just three years ago, hardly anyone in America knew who Jason Priestley was. He arrived in the United States from Canada, where he'd begun his acting career, and while he did land a few small roles, he was virtually unknown. Hollywood is full of would-be stars who double as health-club instructors and waiters in between their sporadic acting jobs. They read the *Hollywood Reporter* and wait for their agents to call. Jason was just another good actor with a rather minor film and television career. But when 90210 was born, Jason's life turned around.

The big question is: who *is* Jason Priestley? What is he *really* like when the cameras stop rolling? Jason is tough, but he is also very gentle. He is cool about his fame and passionate about his work. Some Hollywood performers brag that they have never taken acting lessons. That isn't the case with Jason. He studied acting with several different teachers for years. He is totally dedicated to his craft.

Jason values his privacy, especially regarding his family, so his entire life story has never been fully explored. He possesses a mysterious quality and comes across as "a guy with a secret." You want to know more about him? There's no need to wonder anymore. Here's what you've been waiting for—the Jason Priestley story!

1
IN THE
BEGINNING

Jason's roots are deeply embedded in show business. His maternal grandfather was a circus acrobat and his mother, using the stage name Sharon Kirk, was an actress, choreographer, and ballerina. Yet Jason insists he wasn't pushed into acting; it was, he says, all his own idea.

He was born Jason Bradford Priestley on August 28, 1969, in the beautiful city of Vancouver, British Columbia, Canada. The baby of the family, Jason has one sister, Justine, who is eighteen months older than he. His dad, Lorne, held several jobs while Jason was growing up, from set builder for TV shows and movies to chemist. He now works as a manufacturer's representative for a furniture and textile company.

As a baby, Jason was lovable, cute, funny, and mischievous. He was "a little terror," always getting himself into some kind of trouble. "It seemed like once a week I broke something or got cut," he recalls. "I gave my mother many early heart attacks."

Jason's life up until age three seemed normal and ordinary. He began to talk, walk, and grow teeth at the usual stages, and he had lots of playmates in his neighborhood.

But unlike most children, Jason was introduced to the world of show business. He was practically brought up on the soundstages of the films his mother starred in. She had temporarily interrupted her flourishing acting career to have children, and once they were born, she was ready to go back to work. She had been a popular dancer in Canada, a ballerina who at one time danced two command performances for the queen. In the early 1970s, Sharon was a very successful TV and movie actress in Canada.

When she couldn't find a baby-sitter, she would take her young daughter and baby son with her. One day, on the set of a movie called *A Cold Day in the Park*, the producer was in a frenzy. He needed to find a baby to play Sharon's son but was having difficulty finding one. The solution was simple: Sharon's real-life son would appear in her arms on-screen.

And so Jason Priestley's career began while he was still in diapers, playing a crying baby in his mom's movie *A Cold Day in the Park*. "Right at the very beginning of the movie, there's a shot of a baby crying—that's me!" says Jason, laughing. Even though he doesn't remember that first small taste of acting, it was obvious that show biz was in his blood. The acting bug would officially bite young Jason only four years later.

In the meantime, he enjoyed outings with his close-knit family. They liked to pack up the car and head to the beach or the park. Sometimes when they were out, Sharon would look at her husband and her son and realize how alike they were and how much she loved them both. Sadly, in just a few years, these happy times together would end when Sharon and Lorne divorced, but until then it seemed that Jason and his sister had everything anyone could hope for. "I remember my childhood to be a very happy one," says Jason. "I'm very close to my parents and sister."

Because Sharon was being offered so much work, she found herself away from home a great deal, though she always told her family all about the new role and production she was involved in. Jason would listen intently to her as she explained the details of her new character, and even at the young age of four he expressed a lot of curiosity about acting. Jason didn't just want to know what his mother was doing—he wanted to do it himself! Jason wanted to act.

Jason had always been a little entertainer at home. Whenever his aunts, uncles, and grandparents came over, he'd put on shows for them, and he'd sing and dance. Everyone thought he had loads of talent for such a little boy, but no one, not even his mother, expected him to want to act professionally.

But as Jason got a little older, he was already plotting his career. His sister, Justine, was also interested in acting, and Jason thought they would have a better shot at landing parts if they auditioned as a team. Sharon, however, wanted nothing to do with the idea. She was not a stage mother, and she really didn't want either of her children to embark on acting careers. She felt that they were too young and that it wasn't good for children to have to juggle working with school. Sharon wanted her children to live traditional, carefree kid lives.

But young Jason couldn't shake the acting bug. Even though he also had athletic interests, he really wanted to pursue show business, and he kept after his mother to at least let him give it a try. Having been in the business most of her life, Sharon had seen too many child actors bossed around and controlled by pushy stage mothers. She vowed that when she had kids she would never do that to them, but with Jason hounding her to get him an agent, she wondered if she should break her own rule.

"I begged and begged my mother to get me started," says Jason, who admits he wanted to see if he had what it took, if he had the right stuff to maintain an acting career like his mother.

5

Sharon gave the matter a lot of thought, often coming up with the answer no. She just didn't want Jason to start acting so soon, but at the same time she wondered if she had the right to keep him from at least trying something he really wanted to do, especially knowing that her son did have talent. Sharon was well aware of the fact that if she didn't help Jason now, he'd only try pursuing an acting career on his own later.

Finally, Sharon gave in. She took Jason and Justine to her former agent, who promptly signed them up and sent them out on auditions.

So began the long laborious process of going on auditions and dealing with rejection. For Jason, this has never been a serious problem, probably because he had the support of his family. Surprisingly, Jason learned at a very young age to deal with rejection rationally by shrugging it off and trying again. He knew deep down that if he kept trying, he would eventually be singled out and offered a part.

It didn't take long before casting agents saw the potential in young, personable, talented Jason. He began his career by doing dozens of commercials for all kinds of products, from dog food to toys. It wasn't dramatic acting, but at the age of five, Jason Priestley was certainly on the path he hoped would lead to success. He was in for a bumpy ride but he was definitely headed in the right direction.

2
CHILD STAR

"All actors and actresses have to deal with a whole lot of rejection," says Jason Priestley. "Eventually, though, you become numb to it, and those who persevere and who are willing to plug away at it learn how to deal with it. It's definitely the worst part of acting, but you just have to try to keep it in focus."

Jason kept it "in focus" with the help of his mother, who drove him to all his auditions and watched him adjust to his new surroundings. "My mom would drive me anywhere I had to go," remembers Jason. "But she made me pay her. I used to say to her, 'Why do I have to pay you?' and she would say, 'Well, if I didn't drive you, you'd have to take a cab and you'd have to pay the cab driver.' I was glad that I started to work because otherwise I never would've been able to afford what I was paying my mom," he adds, grinning.

The first two years of Jason's career seemed to go smoothly. He adjusted well to working in commercials and going to school, and his mother was pleased. Even though he occasionally had to leave school for an acting job, Jason wasn't given "star treatment." He went to a public school and hung out with regular kids. "I grew up in the industry, not in the spotlight," he is quick to point out.

The only devastating blow to strike young Jason was the breakup of his parents' marriage. Their divorce when he was just seven years old was painful for both Jason and Justine. They were no longer together as a family, at least not the way they had been, but Jason never believed he was losing either of his parents. They just wouldn't be living together anymore.

Within a few years, both his parents remarried, and Jason found himself with two families. He lived with his mother and stepfather and visited his father on weekends. Jason now also had two stepsisters, his stepmother's daughters, Christine and Karen, and they all seemed to get along.

Jason liked the idea of having so many more people added to his family. "Both my families are great. I love them all!" he reveals. "My biggest worry when I was growing up was what family I should spend Christmas day with!"

While his parents were in the throes of their divorce, Jason put his career on hold. Finding it difficult to concentrate, he stopped auditioning for a few months, but as soon as his home life regained some normalcy he jumped right back into it. After his three-year stint doing only commercials, Jason finally, at age eight, won his first part in the Canadian TV movie Stacey.

His role was small, but it gave him the chance to really act. His mom couldn't help feeling proud of the way he quickly learned his lines and played his part. Even at such a young age, Jason was serious and professional. Everyone on the set liked him and thought he had great potential as an actor. Jason, however, was usually hard on himself, always striving to give a better performance.

"I always hated watching myself on-screen," he says. "I have never been satisfied with any performance I have ever given. But it forces me to improve, which I think is the most important thing. I think the reason I enjoy acting so much is that I can always improve."

Jason soon became a child star in Canada, a boy everyone seemed to recognize either from his countless commercials or from his part in *Stacey*. Sharon came to the realization that Jason wasn't going to quit, or outgrow, acting. Wanting her son to perform to the best of his abilities, she knew he'd need other mentors besides herself, professional drama coaches who could help develop his talent.

Jason started attending acting classes at the Ramona Beauchamp Talent School, and for the first time discovered what it was really like to be an actor. He learned to dig deep within himself and use the events and experiences of his own life to help express the part he was playing. Jason wondered if he could let go of his emotions and pour them all into a role. He loved his acting classes and believed in them, though he admits that actual jobs constitute the real learning process.

"As an actor, I think the best thing to do is work," he asserts. "And as long as you're working, you're learning. You can only learn so much in a classroom. Practical application is far more advantageous. I think experience and learning from other actors is the best way."

It seemed that Jason was on the road to becoming a full-fledged actor, but surprisingly, when he turned eleven, he decided he wanted to stop. He told his mother that acting wasn't for him anymore, that he had other interests now that he was getting older.

After working successfully for six years, Jason Priestley decided to halt his budding career: "I needed time to be a regular kid instead of a Hollywood one who grows up in front of the camera," he says.

But that was only one of his reasons.

3
THE TEENAGE REBEL

According to Jason, he viewed acting differently once he entered junior high school. He felt he was "too old" for the kid roles and "too young" for the teen parts, and being at an awkward age prompted his decision to quit the business.

The main reason he stopped acting, however, was the fact that his friends began teasing him because he was on TV. If he had lived in Hollywood, Jason would have been accepted because there are so many child actors who fill the California classrooms. But in his town, Jason was the only kid in his class who acted and he was being shunned by his classmates because of it. He felt pressured to choose between continuing his career and having friends and a "normal" life.

Jason cared about what the other kids thought, and their teasing really bothered him. He wanted to be part of the crowd, and the only way to do that was to be just like them. He had to dress like them, act like them, and share their interests. But Jason went overboard with his new image—he rebelled against everything and drastically changed his appearance.

Suddenly, he was a kid who got into trouble a lot and spent his spare time hanging out with friends. At age fourteen, he shaved the sides of his head the way the rap stars do today. "It was kind of like a Mohawk," he says. "I didn't want to worry about losing an acting job if I cut off all my hair. I jumped on the tail end of the punk movement. Chains, black jeans, combat boots."

Looking back, Jason sees this time in his life as a "tough period" and his "nonproductive phase." However, he readily admits that "all teenagers go through a change in life, at a time when they're neither adults nor kids. It's during that time that you find out who you are. I just had to find it out myself."

Midway through junior high school, Sharon and her second husband moved her two children to another part of Canada. While most kids find it difficult to leave their friends and start all over again at a new school, Jason considered the move a great adventure. Even though it did take him a while to get used to his new home, experiencing different surroundings and a new school definitely had its advantages. Jason could be anything he wanted to be. No one knew him, he had nothing to prove to anyone, and he could start over in this new place, defining himself in whatever way he chose.

Jason quickly discovered that the missing piece of his personality puzzle seemed to be athletics. He put his energy into playing sports, especially hockey, soccer, and rugby, a sport which Jason describes as "very misunderstood in America."

"I was quite a jock for a while. I was Mr. Athlete!" he says. "I played badminton and

basketball. I ran track and cross-country."
His favorite sport, however, was hockey,
and he even dreamed of playing professionally. But at age sixteen, he knew it would
never happen, even though he was an out-
standing player.

"I wanted to play hockey in the NHL,"
he says. "I finally came to the realization
when I was sixteen that I was not big
enough. I was a pretty good player, but the
NHL was just not going to happen for me."

Regardless of the fact that he would never
be able to play professionally, Jason continued to play hockey all through high school.
In fact, some of his fondest high-school
memories are the hockey games he partici-
pated in. "I got a chance to play once in
Chicago Stadium against the Black Hawks
alumni and that was amazing to me," he
says enthusiastically. "Just being on the ice
playing with those fantastic players was
incredible. I scored a goal in the game."

Jason was never the type to sit on the
sidelines or sit back and wait for things to
happen. When he tackled a project or pur-
sued some activity he always went all the
way. He had so much energy he needed an
outlet, and even though he loved playing
sports, it wasn't enough to satisfy him.

Jason found himself yearning for adventure, for change. He realized that the acting bug had returned, but he was concerned about what his new friends would think of him, especially the guys on the team.

Jason was very confused when he enrolled in the school's drama class and told some team members about his "other" ambitions. Some of them were surprised by his decision.

"You want to be an *actor*?" one member asked incredulously. "Jay, nobody on the team messes with the drama bunch. You can't be in both drama *and* sports."

This experience made him realize something important. He had quit acting to please his classmates in his other school, so that they would accept him. He gave up something he truly loved just because it separated him from the crowd. He realized that he might not have made such a wise decision then—and decided he wanted to satisfy his need for acting now.

Jason decided to disregard what his peers thought about him and to follow his own instincts. He set out to prove them wrong— he knew he could play sports and act in school plays.

Between studying for tests, acting in plays, handing in homework and book reports, and scoring points for the hockey and rugby teams, Jason found time for some good old-fashioned fun. Throughout his teen years, Jason was a boy of many paradoxes. He might retreat to a spot all by himself or mingle with the crowd. He often got straight A's in school, but he liked to pull pranks to get out of classes. His best friend, Steve, was often his partner in mischief.

"We were real practical jokers," Jason says, laughing. "One of our specialties was getting into pretend fights. We'd get thrown out of class, which was exactly what we had in mind!"

One time, during science class, Jason climbed onto a laboratory table and moved the classroom clock ahead forty-five minutes. His teacher was writing the day's assignment on the blackboard, oblivious to what Jason had done. "Excuse me, sir," he called out as the other kids snickered. "It's time to go. I think the bell must be broken."

On another day, Jason and Steve got to class early and stacked all the desks and chairs on top of each other until they reached the room's ceiling. When the classroom started filling up, everyone had quite a job straightening out the two pranksters' work, and most of the period was wasted.

"I drove my teachers crazy!" remembers Jason. "But I got along good with them. I think it was because I always handed in my homework and maintained a good average." It was a well-known fact among his teachers that Jason was an overachiever. They were all used to his endless pranks, but also aware of his academic abilities.

While he still wore his trademark leather jacket, signifying he was a rebel on the outside, Jason was the same serious-minded young man on the inside. He describes himself in his teen years as "a rebel without a clue. It was really strange because I was on the honor roll."

In fact, Jason maintained such high grades, his teachers expected his future to be bright. "In school, I questioned everything," he confesses. "I found out that the secret to learning is questioning what you're hearing, instead of just taking in facts. With subjects like chemistry, physics, or math, there are certain rules you learn, and that's that. But with more subjective classes like history or literature, I think you really have to decide some things for yourself and look deeper than just what you're told."

Because he was so "good at words," many of his English teachers believed he might someday become a writer. However, Mrs. Wrightman, Jason's drama teacher, felt otherwise.

She saw his acting potential from the first day he enrolled in her class. Jason remembers that drama quickly became his favorite school subject and it ultimately made him realize how much he really wanted to act professionally again.

"Mrs. Wrightman was an incredible acting teacher," he says. "I respect her tremendously to this day because she taught us so much about performing and she always treated us like mature people and not like kids."

Throughout high school, Jason preferred to do things his own way. The night of his senior prom is a perfect example of his individualism and nonconformity. Instead of renting a limousine to take him and his date to the prom, Jason talked three of his friends into another means of transportation. He hired a fifty-passenger bus with a driver for the night.

Getting to the prom was a blast, but what happened afterward is Jason's greatest memory of the evening. Some of the other students thought it would be a cool idea to send *their* limousines home and crash Jason's bus. Looking back, he says, "Who would have guessed that the 'party bus' would end up being the highlight of the prom? But that's exactly what it was."

As he neared the end of high school, Jason knew he had to make a quick decision about his future. Even though he had been diligently studying acting, he wasn't absolutely sure that it was the right career move. But as much as Jason tried to move away from it, he kept finding himself drawn right back.

4
BACK TO ACTING

"You did *what?*"

Jason Priestley didn't know whether his mother was happy or angry when he told her what he had done. Without asking her first, he got himself a new agent.

"I didn't know how you'd feel about it," he responded.

But his mom just smiled, gave her son a reassuring hug, and said, "Why didn't you tell me? I'm *thrilled!* You're too talented to just give up."

Jason breathed a sigh of relief. He was

glad his mother supported his decision, because he had already made up his mind. He wasn't going to college; instead, he wanted to pursue acting full time.

He was convinced that working an ordinary job would never suit his personality. While his friends in school were looking forward to graduation and planning their futures in the business world, Jason was setting his sights on what he felt was a more stimulating life, one he felt would give him a great deal of satisfaction.

Jason had received so much encouragement up to this point in his life that he felt he was destined for an acting career. Mrs. Wrightman, his high-school acting teacher, pulled him aside one day after class and told him he should be studying seriously. "She believed in me," says Jason. "And she really gave me a lot of encouragement."

Over the next few years, two more acting coaches would continue to encourage Jason. He began enrolling in several different classes, searching for the right teacher. "While I was still in high school, I took classes all over town and absorbed everything I could," he says. "I even signed up for a jazz dance class so I could learn more about movement."

It wasn't until he crossed paths with the famous drama teacher June Whitaker that Jason began to really learn the most valuable tools of acting. June was a well-respected teacher who was one of the founders of the Neighborhood Playhouse. She quickly became Jason's first and greatest mentor.

"June is really amazing," says Jason. "She brought out so many feelings and skills in me, emotions and talents I never even knew I was capable of."

Of his six acting coaches, Jason credits June with teaching him the most. "No matter how much she taught me, she always had more to give," he recollects. "After applying her techniques to my acting, I'd sometimes find that a method really worked for me and I'd think it was so cool."

While studying with June, Jason soon began to see that acting could be simple. "It's all about finding out what works for you," he reports. "There were times I would try out certain theatrical tips and tricks and realize that they just didn't do it for me."

As Jason became a devoted and enthusiastic drama student, he began making remarkable strides as an actor. His agent, who was based in Los Angeles, began sending him out on auditions for TV shows and films made in Canada. Using the skills he learned from June Whitaker, Jason eagerly began auditioning in the summer following his graduation from high school.

Jason had almost forgotten how grueling auditioning was. "When you're out of it for a while, you forget what it takes to deal with casting agents," he says. "There's so much rejection in this business."

In a business that offers very little compassion, Jason learned fast that he had to put his feelings aside whenever he stepped into a casting agent's office. "If you feel like you have to constantly feel wanted, this business is not for you," he says. "I remember once when I was up for a part, I spent the whole night before studying the lines. I wanted to be so good at the audition. But when I walked in all ready to prove what I could do, they took one look at me and said, 'Thank you, but you're not the type we're looking for.' That was it. They didn't even give me a chance to read for them."

During times like that, it would have been easy for Jason to give up—and understandable if he had. But he didn't. He separated acting from his personal life, and knew that it was just a job. Even though he loved his craft immensely, Jason never let it take over his life. It probably helped that he did not set impossibly high career goals for himself, at least not right away.

"It's a job," he explains. "It doesn't really define who you are as a person. When I lost a part, I just told myself, I'll get the next one I audition for."

That optimistic attitude as well as determination, ambition, and hard work, paid off for Jason. He embarked on a winning streak, landing several roles in TV shows and movies. Jason found himself working at a steady pace in one small role after another. He guest starred in the Canadian-based TV series *Danger Bay*, played Gary in the film *The Boy Who Could Fly*, and then did an episode of *MacGyver*.

"In the beginning, I was basically being cast as the town's bad boy," says Jason. "In *MacGyver*, I was a troubled kid who gets shot at the end. It was really cool because I got to die a long, dramatic death!"

Although his early roles were minor, Jason gave them all he had. He immersed himself in the minds of the characters he played so he could portray them believably.

Even though Jason had been a child actor, this was a brand-new experience. As a child, he didn't pay as much attention to working in front of the cameras, and he remembered his acting in commercials to be exaggerated and easier. The roles he had in *Danger Bay*, *The Boy Who Could Fly*, and especially the *MacGyver* episode gave Jason the opportunity to use his talent in a whole new way. The moving camera became a kind of friend, and he learned to act naturally and subtly in front of it.

Although his career was off to a good start, Jason wasn't satisfied with working only on the screen. He wanted to expand his talents. Most actors who are serious about their craft have a burning desire to perform on the stage. Jason was no exception.

When the offer to do some stage work came his way, Jason jumped at the chance. He played the Judd Nelson role in a local stage production of *The Breakfast Club* and portrayed the James Dean character in *Rebel Without a Cause*. He was also on stage in a play called *Addict*. Acting under the bright lights in a darkened theater before a live audience was an exhilarating experience for Jason. It was demanding, but it gave him room to stretch his talents. He quickly discovered that there is a big difference between stage and screen acting.

"You can never be prepared for what happens on stage because *anything* can happen," he explains. "It's a whole different kind of acting, but very inspiring. For example, if you say a line wrong in a movie or TV show, it's cut out and you do it over. On the stage, you have to cover it up. The stage gives you a chance to improvise and sharpens your skills in that area.

"I never can decide if I like stage or screen better, because I really think I love doing them both," continues Jason. "Each one contains a lot of things which I really enjoy. It's just that they're different."

Jason realized early on the importance of playing different types of roles as well as trying different mediums. "You always have to be trying to improve yourself and improve your craft and continue forward," he says. "I want to keep going and keep improving and keep learning. I think once you stop learning you stagnate."

After graduating from high school, Jason had moved out of his mother's house and was living with his father. He spent one full year commuting back and forth from Canada to Los Angeles for each job and audition, and the traveling was starting to wear him out. "It was getting to be too much," he says. "I was on a plane traveling more than I was working."

At age eighteen, Jason was ready to face new challenges. He was ready to tackle Hollywood and see what tinsel town had to offer. He knew it was a gamble to go out to California when his career was blooming in Canada, but he had saved enough money to get by at least temporarily. With the encouragement of his drama teachers and parents, and the assurance that he was not only good-looking but very talented, Jason's success seemed inevitable.

Jason wanted to move ahead in his career, and he had always known that he might have to move to California. As it was, he wanted to perform in Canadian productions only if they would be shown in America. "It's different in Canada," he says. They don't have a star system like they do in America." And Jason wanted to be a star.

"I knew I had to eventually move to California. I realized I had to live in the town where the work was if I really wanted to succeed," he admits.

In 1987, at the age of eighteen, Jason Priestley said good-bye to his family and friends in Vancouver and set out for Hollywood. Whether or not he would succeed remained to be seen, but he was determined to give it his best shot.

5
NEXT STOP— HOLLYWOOD

Jason's survival skills were put to the test when he left home for California. The first thing he did once he was settled was to start acting classes with the Los Angeles-based drama teacher Howard Fine. Magically, with the help of Fine, he learned to approach his craft in a new way.

"Howard is my favorite teacher of all time," says Jason. "He taught me to interpret any techniques in the roles I play. I learned to use what works for me in each acting situation by taking what I need from the different methods. The ones that don't work, I throw away."

He says Howard taught him "not to bother to analyze too much in a scene. He said spontaneity works best," explains Jason. "That way, it comes as more of an instinctive thing. I was taught a Stanislavsky kind of approach to acting, which is just another description for naturalism or common sense."

Fortunately for him, Jason doesn't have to work long and hard for an emotion to play a scene. "I have what you might call free-flowing emotions," he offers. "I emotionally prepare myself before I attempt a scene. I put myself in the mood and really live out the situation and then I just come up with the rest. I know some actors who take really long to get into the right emotional state but I never really had to do that. I guess I'm very, very lucky."

Jason made some close friends in California, one being David Sherrill, who appeared in *The Rookie*. The two struggling actors shared the rent of a very small, rather run-down apartment, and started pounding the pavement looking for work.

The parts trickled in at a slow but steady

pace for Jason. The first role he won was in an episode of *21 Jump Street*. Ironically, it took him back home to Vancouver, where it was filmed for the Fox Broadcasting Network.

The show would become the biggest factor in determining the future of Jason's career. He was originally cast as bad boy Tober in one episode and was so impressive the producer brought him back for another show. The following season, Jason nabbed the plum role of a teenage alcoholic named Brian on yet another episode of *21 Jump Street*.

With these two roles, Jason was able to play exactly the kind of characters he loved, tough kids who show their vulnerability through plenty of emotion-packed scenes. On the set of *21 Jump Street*, Jason became close pals with the show's stars, Johnny Depp and Richard Grieco.

"Johnny and Richard are both great guys," says Jason, who shared a room with Johnny's stunt double during filming. "We went all over Vancouver together." At the time, heartthrobs Johnny and Richard were taking over as the hottest teen idols in the country. Jason found it strange that everywhere they went, Johnny and Richard were bombarded by girls who wanted to pose with them or get their autographs. As Jason stood off to the side watching them in action, he wondered if he would ever reach that level of success.

"I've never understood actors and actresses who say how much they dislike being recognized," says Jason. "I think it's so flattering. When I became an actor, I knew I was going to give up a certain part of my private life. And, to tell you the truth, it was something I really never minded. Having people compliment you on your work is just an added bonus."

While filming 21 Jump Street, Jason was thrilled to be back on his old stomping grounds. "I never realized how much I missed Vancouver until I really moved away," he says. "It's such a beautiful city. You really get to experience the changing of seasons in Vancouver. I miss the rain, the snow, and watching the leaves turning into autumn colors and falling off the trees. Spring and fall are the most beautiful seasons, but I guess I love Canadian winters most." Unfortunately, Jason would miss the snowfall in Canada that year because he was soon back at work in sunny California.

His 21 Jump Street stint got him some well-deserved attention with the casting people in Hollywood, and he won guest-starring roles on the TV series *Airwolf II*, *The Adventures of Beans Baxter*, and *Quantum Leap*, in all of which he was cast as either a bad boy or a troubled teen. In the *Quantum Leap* episode "The Kamikazi Kid," Jason portrayed a cool member of a street gang.

Next Jason landed a minor part in the 1988 suspense thriller *Watchers*, which starred another young Canadian actor named Corey Haim. The movie was shot in Toronto and centered around a boy named Travis who befriends a magnificent golden retriever that has been given astonishing, humanlike intelligence by a secret government lab. In no time, the boy and his dog are being stalked by a brutal monster, also developed by the government.

Corey Haim played Travis, while Jason played a minor part. Unfortunately, Jason got his first bitter taste of disappointment when his big final scene ended up on the cutting-room floor.

"At the end of the movie, I got killed by a monster," he says. "But at the last minute the director decided not to include my dying scene. I was so upset."

He didn't have too much time to think about the disappointment, though, because he immediately began working on other projects once filming for *Watchers* ended. He won parts in the film *Nowhere to Run* and the TV movies *Lies from Lotus Land* and *Nobody's Child*. As luck would have it, Jason arrived in Hollywood shortly before the writers' strike, which caused mass cancellations of productions and left many actors unemployed. Jason wasn't immune to the effects of the strike, and he found himself losing roles as fast as he had been winning them. He was out of work for the better part of one full year.

"I don't know what happened," he says. "One day my agent stopped calling. I wasn't prepared for it, but I'm sure it happens to every young actor."

At nineteen years old, Jason was homesick and in debt. Even though his career was drastically declining, he never saw this period in his life as a time to quit. "I never once thought I should give up and go to college," he says.

With so many roles already under his

belt, he felt he had an excellent start on a steady career as an actor. He knew there would be more roles—but when? It was almost as if his seriousness and commitment to the business were being tested. "The real secret to making it in this business is to have enough ambition and drive," he says. "If you can stick it out through the ups and downs, I think you can rise above it."

Of course, Jason had no idea if he was actually going to make it in show business. The odds are stacked against aspiring actors, but Jason was fortunate enough to have talent, good looks, and ambition, all the necessary ingredients for succeeding in the industry. The rest is hard work, perseverance, and luck. Even though Jason had been working in Canada and a brief stint in Hollywood, it seemed like it was time for him to pay his dues.

Jason's agent sent him on one frustrating audition after another, and gradually Jason learned to survive his bleak situation. Although his savings started to dwindle, he tried not to panic. In fact, he lived it up the first few months he was unemployed, probably assuming that the dry spell would be over quickly. Now he looks back on it as "the most fun I ever had in my life. My friend and I had this car, a 1968 Cadillac Coupe DeVille. This car was huge and we used to drive it around town. We lived in this little North Hollywood apartment and called the car our Homesmobile. It was a wild time!"

When his money finally did run out, Jason returned to Vancouver for six months. He credits his mom with helping him through this uncertain period in his life. "My mom taught me to be independent and self-reliant from a very early age," he says. "And that has given me the strength to deal with the craziness of this business."

Jason returned to California, and once the writers' strike was over, he started landing a few roles. The first part he was offered was in the film *Caddo Lake*. This job holds a very special place in his heart because he got his mother a role in it as well.

A few years earlier, Sharon had unexpectedly had to leave show business because she snapped a hamstring while dancing. She decided to pursue a career in real estate, but the desire to act never left her, and Jason knew that.

When he arrived on the set of *Caddo Lake*, he discovered that the role of his mother had not yet been cast. "I told the producer that my mom was an actress and he told me to tell her about the role," says Jason. "The next thing I knew she had the part and was on a plane to California."

By getting his mom a role in *Caddo Lake* Jason felt that he was thanking her for helping to launch his career. It was the first time Sharon and Jason had played mother and son on-screen since his big debut as the crying baby in her film *A Cold Day in the Park*.

With *Caddo Lake*, Jason was back on the acting track. His next role was that of saintly guardian angel Buzz Gunderson, who comes down to earth from heaven to help teens through rough times, in the two Disney Channel movies *Teen Angel* and *Teen Angel Returns*. The two films were broken down into fifteen-minute segments and shown in succession on new episodes of *The Mickey Mouse Club*.

There was no question that with every role he played, Jason was one step closer to where he wanted to be. But everything he had played so far was either supporting or guest-starring. Only the *Teen Angel* movies utilized more of his talents, and Jason wasn't completely satisfied with the direction of his career. He hadn't yet been offered the part that would make his name a household word. He knew his "big break" was out there somewhere; he just had to sit tight and play the waiting game a little while longer.

6
RACING TO STARDOM

Nineteen eighty-nine would be an incredibly momentous year for Jason Priestley. Fed up with playing minor roles in TV shows and films, he decided he was ready to audition for a series. If he was lucky enough to get onto a regular show, it would mean steady work, steady money, and regular, weekly exposure.

When auditions for the new television season began, he was ready to read for any role at any open call in town. He made the rounds and lost nearly everything he tried out for. But his luck would change at the audition for a new show called Sister Kate.

The producers had already auditioned five or six other actors for the role of Todd Mahaffey, but no one seemed right. When Jason read, they knew he was perfect for the role. He made a strong first impression, and they had a feeling they would give him the part, though they didn't show Jason much encouragement after his first reading.

They told him his test was excellent and that they'd be in touch. Jason assumed that that was their way of telling him that he hadn't gotten the part. Even though the producers of Sister Kate were convinced they wouldn't find another young actor better suited for the part than Jason, surprisingly, they kept looking.

"I had a feeling I didn't read as well as I should have," Jason later revealed. "By the time I did that audition, I was completely exhausted, and I think it showed."

He was upset with himself because he saw the role as a real challenge, a great opportunity, and he wanted it very badly. "At first, I thought it was going to be a good role for an actor to play," says Jason. As a starring role in an ensemble cast, he thought it would show off his talents.

He waited one week, and when he didn't hear back from the producers, he decided to chalk it off as just another disappointment.

Then, about two weeks later, his agent called with good news. The producers of *Sister Kate* wanted to see him again. Jason dashed over to their office that same afternoon, and before he left he was officially cast in the role of Todd Mahaffey. Later, Jason's agent told him he had set an auditioning record. Usually actors audition six or seven times before a producer commits to a final decision, but they were so impressed with Jason that he had to audition only twice.

Jason was eager to play a part that was so different not only from his own personality but also from the types of roles he had been accustomed to playing. Welcoming the change, Jason was quoted as saying, "I think the worst thing for an actor is being typecast. I'm happy that I'm being given the chance to play a variety of roles."

The role of Todd was that of a teenage orphan who was good-hearted and not very bright. Jason often described the character as "the big brother. He sees and understands everything, but when it comes to schoolwork, he's not exactly a rocket scientist. He's a good guy; the only reason he hasn't been adopted is because he's so old, and people want to adopt babies. He's been bounced around the system a little bit. He's been in lots of foster homes that never seem to work out for him."

The format of *Sister Kate*, as outlined by press releases before the 1989–90 TV season got under way, struck many critics as being that of a predictable flop. Since it was a season in which the industry was placing much emphasis on the buying power of young viewers, it came as no surprise that this new series would feature a cast consisting largely of kids.

It aired on Sunday nights on NBC in the eight-to-eight-thirty time slot. The season premiere did not receive good reviews or a large share of the ratings, and it seemed as if Jason's first big break was doomed before it even started. But NBC wasn't going to kill *Sister Kate* without giving it full support and a chance to succeed.

Reviews of the show seemed unanimous. "Did you hear the one about the funny nun?" wrote one critic. "She had seven kids—all orphans. Okay—it's not funny, but it *is* the premise of *Sister Kate*, a new half-hour comedy."

Perhaps *Sister Kate* might have worked better if it were a drama, but as a comedy it fell flat. Stephanie Beacham, who was coming right from her stint on *Dynasty*, played Sister Kate, a hard-boiled nun who comes to restore order among seven rebellious, unruly orphans. Jason led the group of likable actors who portrayed the orphans; the other kids in the cast were newcomers Erin Reed, Hannah Cutrona, Penina Segall, Harley Cross, Alexaundria Simmons, and Joel Robinson.

The action took place inside Redemption House, a Catholic residence for children, and the basic theme of the show was how the kids discouraged prospective parents from adopting them. In show after show, they did whatever they could to stay together. They even managed to scare off the last three priests who cared for them before Sister Kate arrived.

Jason didn't mind working on *Sister Kate*, but he wasn't too fond of his character. "I'm waiting for them to develop Todd a little better," he revealed in an interview. "My character has the IQ of a bag of dirt and I'd really like to see him get a bit smarter. Even though he's a tough guy, he has some visible tenderness underneath."

Unfortunately, the writers never had the chance to develop Jason's role. The show didn't last long enough. When it was canceled, after only a few months on the air, Jason had mixed emotions. Even though he described the role of Todd as "one-dimensional and slow-minded," it did help Jason to gain recognition. The talent directory *Faces International* named Jason one of the "Hot New Faces of 1990." Getting by on his adorable good looks, he also started to receive press coverage in teen magazines. He was finally beginning to get national recognition as one of the nation's hottest new teenage actors when *Sister Kate* was canceled. This new hitch in his career left him feeling very frustrated.

Later, he would say in an interview that what he especially enjoyed about working on *Sister Kate* was the feeling of team play from the other actors. "I liked working with an ensemble cast," he said. "Everyone is fantastic. The producers, writers, the art director, and all the actors work well together. It all really jells when you're working as a team. That makes it easy!"

By the spring of 1990, Jason was itching to get back to work. He knew he wanted to try out for another role in a television series and he started gearing himself up for auditions again. He would later find out that he never had to worry where his next acting job was going to come from—he didn't even have to leave his home. The role of a lifetime was on its way to Jason's doorstep, and his wish to work on another series would be granted sooner than he expected.

7

THE HIT SHOW— *BEVERLY HILLS, 90210*

Jason was out looking for work after the demise of *Sister Kate* when on the other side of town twenty-nine-year-old Darren Star was putting the finishing touches on a treatment for a new show, *Class of Beverly Hills*. He hoped to get it on the air for the 1990 fall season, but it was a lot to wish for, especially since Darren Star wasn't a television writer. A graduate of the University of California, where he majored in English and creative writing, Star's previous credits were screenplays for the films *If Looks Could Kill*, starring Richard Grieco, and *Doin' Time on Planet Earth*. He had no plans to stop working on movie scripts, but as he was flipping around the channels on TV one night, he noticed there was something missing. There were no shows about real teenagers. "Most shows for adolescents seem like they are written by fifty-year-olds who think teenagers behave like seven-year-olds," Star says.

He set out to fill that important gap by creating an honest show about high school, one that would deal with real, everyday issues. At the time, he saw it as "a *Thirtysomething* for teens."

"In high school, everything is so important and so serious," he says. "There wasn't a show that addressed that mind-set. Nobody had done a really quality drama about high school. One that didn't condescend, that was not a sitcom, that took the teenage audience on its own terms. I thought Beverly Hills would be a good hook for this kind of show."

He sat down at his word processor and began banging out what resulted in the show's pilot. It was different and well-written. The premise of the one-hour drama focused on twin teens Brandon and Brenda Walsh, who move with their values-oriented, middle-class family from Minnesota to posh Beverly Hills. Back in Minneapolis, Brandon, who is three minutes older than Brenda, was very popular, and now he finds himself in a high school filled with the privileged children of celebrities and tycoons, who drive to school in Porsches and BMWs.

No one was interested in Star's idea or his script. The three big networks—ABC, NBC, and CBS—all turned it down. The only place left to turn was the Fox Broadcasting Network, which was only five years old but had an impressive track record.

Multimillionaire Rupert Murdoch was the mastermind behind launching the Fox Broadcasting Network. The owner of magazines, newspapers, and radio and TV stations was hoping to compete with ABC, NBC, and CBS. No one who had ever tried it before had been successful; Murdoch was going to be the first.

The baby network started small, airing shows only on Saturday and Sunday nights. In the fall of 1986, it had its first three shows on the air: *Married . . . With Chil-*

dren, *The Tracey Ullman Show*, and 21 *Jump Street*. From the start, Fox had a soft spot for shows about teens. Since teenagers make up the largest percentage of the viewing public, a large majority of Fox's shows catered to a young audience. The shows on Fox painted a realistic portrait of teenage life.

That might have been the reason they expressed so much interest in *Class of Beverly Hills*. They bought Star's pilot, added it to their fall lineup, and began looking for a producer to undertake this new project.

Enter Aaron Spelling, the head of a production company that has been responsible for some of the biggest commercial hits in TV history, including *Dynasty*, *The Mod Squad*, *Charlie's Angels*, and *The Love Boat*. High school was not a theme Spelling was familiar with. Yet even though none of his previous series devoted airtime to teenagers, Fox wanted Spelling.

"Fox called and said, 'Would you like to do a high-school show?' and I said, 'Not particularly,' " recalls Spelling. "I said that I don't know how to do *Ferris Bueller's Day Off* and *Parker Lewis Can't Lose*. They said, 'No, we'd like to do a show in Beverly Hills, with strangers from a foreign land like Minnesota coming to it.' I said, 'That's intriguing.' I really got excited."

A copy of Star's pilot script was sent to Spelling. He read it and immediately started thinking about the casting. It was mutually understood that the cast would be a group of relative unknowns. Spelling and Fox were more concerned with finding talent than stars. The people connected with the show figured from the beginning that they'd make their own stars—after all, who knew Johnny Depp or Richard Grieco before their success on the Fox network?

Casting began in the spring of 1990, and it was no easy task. Hundreds of young actors and actresses poured in and out of the auditions, hoping to land one of the parts. As the roles were slowly being cast, it seemed the biggest problem was finding two actors to portray the show's twins, the lead roles, Brandon and Brenda Walsh. Aaron Spelling was at a complete loss; no one he was interviewing seemed to fit either role. He decided to turn to his teenage daughter, Tori, for some help.

Tori had read the script for the pilot episode and loved it. "I couldn't believe what

Jason and his 90210 costars Shannen Doherty and Luke Perry were presenters at the 43rd Annual Emmy Awards.

(Copyright © 1991 by John Paschal/Celebrity Photo)

Jason with his Sister Kate cast mates
left to right) Penina Segall, Hannah Cutrona,
Alexaundria Simmons, and Erin Reed.
(Copyright © 1989 by John Paschal/Celebrity Photo)

The eyes have it! Jason's eyes are blue and
beautiful and sensitive, too.

(Copyright © 1989 by Greg De Guire/Celebrity Photo)

Jason has been dating actress Robyn Lively on and off for the past two years.

(Copyright © 1991 by Scott Downie/Celebrity Photo)

Jason and the cast of Sister Kate *made one last appearance together at the Hollywood Christmas Parade in 1989 before the show was cancelled.*

(Copyright © 1989 by Scott Downie/Celebrity Photo)

In high school, Jason wore his trademark leather jacket every day. But he says, "I was a rebel without a clue. It was really strange because I was on the honor roll."

(Copyright © 1989 by Dan Golden/Shooting Star)

"I didn't grow up in the spotlight," says
Jason. *"I went to a regular school. I played
hockey and did all of the normal kid things."*
(Copyright © 1990 by Aubrey Reuben/London Features
USA)

Jason and costar Shannen Doherty, the world's most popular twin teens, on the hit TV series Beverly Hills, 90210 are all dressed up for the Emmy Awards.

(Copyright © 1991 by Scott Downie/Celebrity Photo)

When Jason isn't working, he pops out the contact lenses he wears for the show and puts on his favorite pair of glasses.

(Copyright © 1990 by Greg De Guire/Celebrity Photo)

Photographers snap Jason wherever he goes—even at the supermarket!
(Copyright © 1991 by Angie Coqueran/ London Features USA)

Fun and friendship are priorities to Jason, who happily posed with Khrystyne Haje (left) and Robyn Lively (right) at a Hollywood party.

(Copyright © 1990 by Roman Salicki/Shooting Star)

Jason Priestley at the 1991 MTV Video Music Awards.

(Copyright © 1991 by John Paschal/Celebrity Photo)

Jason loves the outdoors—playing hockey, riding his motorcycle, hanging out with his closest friends.

(Copyright © 1989 by John Paschal/Celebrity Photo)

Jason is a hero with a heart of gold who volunteers his time for numerous charity events. He played softball for the T. J. Martell Foundation and helped raise $400,000 for children with cancer, AIDS, and leukemia. *(Copyright © 1991 by Darlene Hammond/Archive Photos)*

"*Jason is never negative,*" *raves Brian Austin Green (David on 90210). "He's a real positive influence.*"

(*Copyright © 1991 by John Paschal/Celebrity Photo*)

At the MTV Video Music Awards, Jason and copresenter Jennifer Connelly (of The Rocketeer) had a blast posing for photographers.

(Copyright © 1991 by Tammie Arroyo/Celebrity Photo)

Concerning his future, Jason says, "I'd like to become a director and writer someday, but I'm in no hurry. I plan to be in this business for a long time."

(Copyright © 1989 by John Paschal/Celebrity Photo)

a real show it was," she explains. "I told my dad how great I thought it was. I knew it would be a good show."

As the daughter of one of TV's most famous producers, Tori grew up surrounded by Hollywood. "When I was younger, my dad used to take me to cast parties," she says. "I grew up on the sets of his shows. I was always meeting stars and I wanted to be part of show business from the time I was really young."

Tori had been given roles in some of her dad's series. As a teenager, she began polishing her acting skills and continued appearing on TV until making her feature-film debut in *Troop Beverly Hills* with Shelley Long. It's no surprise that she became tight with many teenage actors and often suggested some of them to her dad when he was casting a new project.

When the question of casting Brenda and Brandon Walsh came up, Tori knew the perfect actors for the roles. "I had never met Shannen Doherty, but I had seen her in the movie *Heathers* and on the TV show *Our House*," says Tori. "I thought she was a really good actress and told my dad to audition her for the role of Brenda."

When Shannen got the call to audition for the show, she was leery. After *Our House*, she had been sent scripts for new series but hated everything. Even though she wanted to work, she just didn't want to play the teenage daughter in a half-hour sitcom. The honesty of Brenda Walsh appealed to Shannen, and the premise of the show was almost like a dream come true. She auditioned and won the role.

Finally, they had an actress to play Brenda—now they had to find Brandon. Tori put her thinking cap back on and visually pictured the actor she thought should play Brandon Walsh. The actor she had in mind was Jason Priestley. She says, "He's just gorgeous. He has the most beautiful blue eyes I've ever seen. I remember seeing him on *Sister Kate* and I had the biggest crush on him."

Three days before the pilot was to begin filming, Tori told her dad to contact Jason and interview him.

When Jason's agent called to send him on the audition for what was being called "a new Aaron Spelling show," his first reaction was, "Wow, when I was growing up, every show I watched was an Aaron Spelling show."

He went in and read for the role on a Thursday, was cast, and began learning his lines that same night. On Monday morning at six o'clock sharp, he was on the set of his second TV series ready to start playing his brand-new, character, Brandon Walsh. Before he delved deep into his new role, he had to meet the other actors who also would be in the show. Jason was happy to learn that he knew some of them.

When the auditions were being held for *90210*, Tori Spelling had secretly tried out for the role of Kelly Taylor. She didn't nab that role but did get the part of Donna, who is style-conscious and "concerned with money, shopping, and parties," as Tori puts it.

The actress who was cast as Kelly, the leader of the hip brat pack at West Beverly Hills High, was Jennie Garth. Before *90210*, she had appeared in the short-lived TV series *A Brand New Life* with Barbara Eden and had made guest appearances on *Growing Pains* and *Circus of the Stars*. She was also in the Disney Channel movie *Teen Angel Returns*, where she first met and worked with Jason Priestley.

The role of the reserved and intellectual

Andrea Zuckerman went to Gabrielle Carteris, who had appeared on the New York stage and studied acting with the Royal Academy of Dramatic Art and the London Academy of Music and Dramatic Art. Gabrielle had had roles in three *After School Specials*, "What If I'm Gay?," "Seasonal Differences," and "Just Between Friends." She also played a repeat role in the soap *Another World* and appeared in the movie *Jackknife*. Gabrielle, who was glad to be working with Jason, says, "We were friends before we started working on the show. He's a great guy, and he kisses fine, too. But we're just close friends. I only kiss Jason when we're doing a scene together!"

Brian Austin Green is a popular young actor. Having appeared in a string of TV and film roles including that of Brian Cunningham on *Knots Landing*, he says he was "bitten by the acting bug at age eleven." He won the plum role of David Silver on *90210*, and describes him as a "guy who will do anything to be part of the in crowd."

"I'm similar to David in that I'm kind of girl crazy," says Brian. "But our motives are different. I personally wouldn't do a lot of the things he does."

Ian (pronounced "eye-an") Ziering describes his role of Steve Sanders as "egotistical, spoiled, rich, and sometimes a real arrogant kid. Steve really doesn't know any boundaries." Ian, who began acting at an early age when a talent manager spotted him in a grocery store, has appeared in three soap operas (*Love of Life*, *The Guiding Light*, and *The Doctors*), one movie (*Endless Love*), and the Broadway musical *I Remember Mama*. A New Jersey native, he was cast for the California-based show in New York City.

Last, but certainly not least, is Luke Perry, who joined the cast midway through the 1990 season as the mysterious Dylan McKay. Luke says his character is a "staggering intellect who understands enough about human nature to know you don't have to be physical to be intimidating." Luke, who grew up on a farm in Fredericktown, Ohio, got his first break in acting playing Ned Bates on the soap *Loving* and followed that up with the recurring role of Kenny on *Another World*. He says 90210 is "the best show on television, except for *Jeopardy!*" and hates it when people compare him to James Dean. "It's just a bad hairline," he says. "Everyone's been compared to James Dean—even Michael J. Fox."

Rounding out the cast are Carol Potter and James Eckhouse as Cindy and Jim Walsh. The show also boasts a large creative team of quality writers, directors, and producers. Steve Wasserman and Jessica Klein, who have written for *Northern Exposure*, are the series story editors; Charles Rosin, the supervising producer of *Northern Exposure* last season, is the executive producer; Charles Braverman and Tim Hunter are the directors; and creator Darren Star serves as supervising producer and writer of a few episodes.

Jason especially liked the idea of being part of an ensemble team just like he had been on *Sister Kate*.

He was enthusiastic about the show and his role as the Minnesota-raised teenager, learning to cope with life in Beverly Hills. "There are a lot of shows that make high school out to be a wonderful place," says Jason. "But really kids today face a lot of serious problems, and we feel our show is very aware of these issues. We've tried to address them honestly."

Jason found his character to be stimulating and interesting to play. "I don't think I am like Brandon, but I can identify with him in a lot of ways, especially the fact that he moved to California from Minnesota. That parallels my own life, only I came from Vancouver. A lot of things that Brandon first saw when he came to town were the first things I saw when I first arrived in L.A."

He describes Brandon as "a normal guy thrust into the glamorous, fast-paced lifestyle of Beverly Hills. He wants to fit in, but he's secure enough with who he is not to let go of his midwestern values and morals."

From the beginning, Jason admitted that Brandon was more fun to play than his last series role of Todd on *Sister Kate*. "I liked playing Todd, but Brandon is more of a challenge. He's a lot deeper. He's operating on more levels than Todd was."

The season premiere, on Thursday, October 18, 1990, at 9:00 P.M., didn't generate a lot of interest from viewers, nor did it receive good reviews from critics. One reviewer wrote that the show contained "stereotypes and stock characters." Another said, "The Walshes are just another family to go from a small town to Beverly Hills. The Clampetts had already traveled the same route in *The Beverly Hillbillies*." And then there was the reviewer who reported, "If the writers [of *90210*] cut some of the whining messages, stereotypes, and overlong scenes, they might have a winner—though opposite *Cheers*, it's unlikely."

In the early reviews, Jason was the only one being singled out and receiving positive notices. Critics who didn't praise the show were applauding his performance. One magazine said, "At least Priestley, wasted on *Sister Kate* last season, is a shoo-in to make Fox's young female audience forget Richard Grieco and Johnny Depp."

The producers were happy with their star. As for the show, they decided the original title *Class of Beverly Hills* had to be changed. They blamed the poor reviews on the title and changed it to *Beverly Hills, 90210*—the numbers being the zip code for Beverly Hills. When the show became *the* program to watch, it would simply be known to fans as *90210*.

Darren Star figured the name change would solve the show's slow climb up the ratings chart. "I think it was perceived as a glitzy, insubstantial show about Beverly Hills because of the original title," he says. "The zip-code title was supposed to widen the appeal to adults. Now I'm used to it. People think the title is strange, but it's caught on because of that."

In December 1990, after only one and a half months on the air, the ratings for *90210* were so low it was on the brink of cancellation. In fact, it seemed to be one of Fox's only real flops of the new season. But the powers that be involved with *90210* weren't going to watch it fall into oblivion.

The show's executive producer, Charles Rosin, says, "We were so marginal for so long. We went to the Fox network and said, 'Listen, unless you start promoting us, no one's going to know we're here.' Lucky for them, Fox had enough faith in the show to listen and start a promotional campaign. They were also lucky Fox had nothing else to put in its place, otherwise *90210* would've been history. By giving it another chance and keeping it on the air, the show began making history."

"It was to our advantage that Fox doesn't have a backlog of shows it can slide in if one show is not performing," says Star. "We had the luxury of letting the audience find us. We felt we would really catch on in reruns, and that's pretty much what happened."

By February 1991 the show was in the number-two position behind *Cheers* for Thursday night. By April, teenagers around the world were faithfully tuning in every week to see what was new in the lives of Brandon, Brenda, and their rich Beverly Hills friends. By May, *90210* was being hailed as Fox's teen sleeper hit of the year, with Jason, Shannen Doherty, and Luke Perry being named three of the year's most exciting and personable new stars. By June, *90210* was drawing more teenage viewers than any of its Thursday-night rivals, including *Cheers.*

It was clear that the secret to *90210*'s success was a combination of two very important things: the incredibly cute and talented cast and the way the episodes have dealt in a mature way with teenage sexuality, drinking and driving, AIDS, parental abuse of drugs, breast cancer, divorce, date rape, and a host of other issues that confront teens.

Says Darren Star, "We always try to avoid being consciously hip. What carries the show are stories that are dramatic and interesting. We're not coining the latest teen lingo. Being a teenager is universal; you can be any age and still tap into what it's like."

At the end of nearly every show that deals with a social issue there is information and practical advice for kids experiencing similar problems. Wherever available, a toll-free phone number flashes across the screen so viewers can contact the appropriate organization dealing with the issue featured in that week's episode.

The producers do not simply want the show to be mindless entertainment, but rather a caring, thought-provoking drama, whose main mission is to reach out to its viewers.

As Aaron Spelling points out, "The problems of young people have accelerated and so have their feelings and thoughts. We had the guts to make Luke Perry be a member of AA. And we had Jason, our star, drinking and driving. That's reality."

The fan mail Jason and the cast receive is proof positive of the kind of effect the show is having on its loyal following. "I get letters all the time from kids who tell me how much they can relate to an episode," says Jason. "They write in to tell me how the show helped them. I think the reason why we've been successful is because we're not preachy when we address these subjects. We're not saying don't do this or that. We simply devote one hour to an important issue and show what the possible effects can be."

Probably the most important place for the show to catch on is with the kids who attend Beverly Hills High, which is the inspiration for 90210's fictitious West Beverly Hills High. But some students set out to discourage others in the school from watching it before really knowing what the show was all about. The student newspaper, Highlights, began running a steady flow of articles saying 90210 was a joke. It was only after stories became increasingly serious and real and girls wanted to check out Jason and series costar Luke Perry that the school got serious about it. Now the skeptics never miss an episode, and some students have started Club 90210.

After playing Brandon for one full season, Jason Priestley had absolutely no complaints. He was starring on a hot hit TV series and was loving every minute of it. "I got a soft spot in my heart for Brandon," he says. "I don't think there is anyone who knows Brandon better than I do. I'm having a great time with him!"

8

ON THE SET WITH THE *90210* GANG

During the first season of *90210*, Jason couldn't have been more pleased with his increasing popularity. "I'm just excited. I'm getting a lot of respect as an actor. Not just as a teen idol, which is great fun, but I'm getting respect as an actor and that's nice."

As he made his way around the talk-show circuit, everyone was congratulating Jason on his success. Arsenio Hall, showing a stack of magazines with Jason's face on the covers, said, "You *are* hot!" And Faith Daniels of *A Closer Look* became the envy of teenagers who work at NBC for the summer. When she talked to Jason via satellite, she told him, "Thanks for making me cool with the interns."

Jason finally was getting the recognition he deserved, but he wasn't about to take the spotlight away from the rest of the cast. After all, 90210 is an ensemble show, and even though he was being singled out, it's the work of everyone combined that helps to make the show a hit.

If you pay close attention to 90210, you can see how easily and comfortably the cast works together. The fact that no one is given more star treatment than the other is a primary reason for their on- and off-camera comaraderie. Each cast member has his or her own personalized director's chair, and for location filming, they are each given his or her own trailer.

In April, when 90210 vaulted into Neilsen's top forty, Fox had a brainstorm. They decided to keep the viewers tuned in all summer by ordering seven brand-new episodes. This is something that has never been done before in television. All shows film twenty-three episodes a year and then take a three-month hiatus before beginning the new season. Fox decided *Beverly Hills, 90210's second* season would begin in July, and instead of the usual twenty-three episodes, they ordered thirty fresh new shows.

Aaron Spelling's reaction was, "It's a gamble, but I'll tell you, they've got guts."

The show zoomed into the top twenty and was the most watched series in the summer of 1991.

What is a typical day on the set of *90210* really like? For one thing, it begins around 6:00 A.M. and lasts until well past 10:00 P.M. Because there are so many cast members, not all the actors work together everyday. It depends on who is given the bigger role for each show. Generally, in total, they do forty-five pages of dialogue every week. It is a grinding schedule for the cast, but especially grueling for Jason, who, as the star, usually has the most dialogue and often, with Shannen, works the longest hours.

Filming *90210* is a very slow process. Learning their lines and perfecting their roles are just part of the actors' jobs. Just as much time goes into choosing the right wardrobe for each actor, getting their hair done, and putting on makeup.

The set, which is in Van Nuys, California, is a hectic place where everyone, cast and crew, usually dashes about in different directions. Hours can drag on and on, especially during rehearsals, when they must do the same scene over and over. That can certainly make for short tempers. Shannen realistically explains, "Being on the set sixteen hours a day, sometimes I get very stressed out. You do not work those kind of hours and not start feeling it. When I start to feel tired, I don't want to be rude, so I go into my dressing room, put on some music, and call my girlfriends on the phone."

With no hiatus, the work load proved to be so much for the cast that Jennie nearly collapsed on the set in June and had to be rushed to the hospital. She was quickly released.

During the times when he is waiting to film his scenes, Jason keeps himself busy by reading his script, giving a quick interview to a magazine, talking on the phone to his agent, or checking out the day's fan mail. His favorite pastime, however, is playing Game Boy, the hand-held video game.

The happy family of young stars spend their spare time on the set giggling with one another, hugging, and kissing. Most of them try not to let the long hours get them down; they do a great job of keeping their spirits up even late into the night. It was said that director Charles Braverman at ten o'clock one Friday night had to tell his enthusiastic cast, "All right, guys, tense up. Time to shoot the scene."

Gabrielle, or Gabby, as her friends call her, exclaims, "Everyone in the cast is so different, but we work well together because we respect one another. It's always so much fun to shoot scenes together as a group. We don't work together at the same time very often, so when we do, it's very exciting. I think that's why my favorite episode was the show about the prom. We all were together for one week."

Because the cast members are all friends, they enjoy working as a team, and that helps to get their job done. There's never a big problem of anyone having a big ego, because everyone is professional. They seem to leave all their personal feelings at home; once they get on the set and the cameras start rolling, they are all concerned with putting together the best show possible. The group even has lunch, and sometimes dinner, together.

It would be understandable if Jason and Luke Perry were offscreen rivals. But they get along great. "On our show Brandon and Dylan share an equal fifty-fifty relationship in which they learn a lot from each other," says Jason. "I'm happy to say that Luke and I have a similar friendship off the set."

Luke agrees, adding, "Jay's my partner in crime. He's one of the best actors I have ever worked with. I would have been friends with him even if we didn't work together, because we are a lot alike."

Most actors, especially those in fierce competition with each other, might want to go in the opposite direction on nonworking days. But these two thrill seekers often spend their days hanging out together. They're even planning a trip together if they ever get a break in their schedules. "We want to go to Juarez, a crazy little town in Mexico," Jason says, smiling. "It's just over the Texas border, and it is a wild and fun place to cut loose."

Jason's favorite way to relieve the stress of popularity is bungee jumping—and he got Luke interested in it, too. High on a bridge in the Angeles National Forest, north of L.A., Jason and Luke are getting set to jump. Harnesses strap their waists to a bungee cord on top of the bridge. They close their eyes for a second, and then plunge down—*waaaaaay* down—and then up again! Jason says of the experience, "You jump off and the first thing you think of is, 'I've just willingly committed suicide!'" It's certainly not something Fox and Spelling want to hear from their bankable star. If they could keep Jason locked in a room, they would—just to ensure his absolute safety at all times.

Recently, Ian Ziering joined his costars in their on-the-set pranks. Gabrielle calls Ian "the funniest guy on the set. He's always cracking me up." Surely, his practical jokes are running neck in neck with Jason's and Luke's. "But," said another cast member, "I think when it comes to who plays the most practical jokes, Jason gets the crown as king of the pranksters."

Jason is famous for trying to crack up the other actors during a tense scene. He is a perpetual jokester; no one on the set is safe from his mischief. He says it helps him. Jason loosens up by acting wild and crazy. His approach is different from some of the other cast members. While they need an hour or more of concentration to get themselves into their characters, Jason seems to need only a few minutes. When the director yells "action," he's ready to roll into the life of Brandon Walsh without so much as a moment to think about it.

His scenes usually only require two or three takes. He gets fidgety if it takes longer. Director Charles Braverman says, "With Jason it's very easy and cool almost all the time."

Aaron Spelling says, "Jason's been our quarterback, keeping everybody on an even keel."

While teenagers in America and England were spending the summer of 1991 enjoying the 90210 kids' summer vacation, a line of merchandise from the show was being planned. The line includes clothes for juniors (now they can dress just like Brenda, Donna, Kelly, and Andrea), as well as a complete line of T-shirts, beach towels, posters, notebooks, and more.

None of this hoopla seems to do much for Jason. He doesn't pay too much attention to the show's ratings or the products. He doesn't get involved in the business side of his job at all; he is only concerned with his character and what Brandon should or shouldn't be getting himself into.

"I try not to pay attention to the numbers," he says. "I don't like anything distracting from my focus and what I'm doing. I try not to worry about the politics involved. I'm just interested in the character and what is being said on the show."

He doesn't always agree with what the writers are doing with his character and he questions them quite a bit, as does the rest of the cast, most notably Shannen. Perhaps part of the show's appeal is the fact that the actors actually care about what their characters have to say every week. They don't all just read their lines, they live them, and hope they are conveying the right message to the teens who are watching. Because the actors feel so comfortable in their roles, they don't hesitate to question the writers when they aren't particularly happy with a certain scene. Sometimes it does some good, sometimes it doesn't, but at least they give it a try.

"I've been playing Brandon for so long, I am very used to him. Things happen, and I say, 'Brandon wouldn't do it that way. He'd probably do it this way.' " Luckily for Jason, the writers and producers welcome the input from their actors, even if they don't always change the script to suit the star.

Shannen explains that she really wasn't too happy with the controversial episode titled "Spring Dance" where Brenda lost her virginity. "When I read the script, I wasn't too thrilled about it," she says. "I didn't want that to happen to Brenda and I mentioned it to the producer. We have a whole cast that is sexually active—almost all of the characters except mine. I didn't think Brenda should go to bed with someone she's been seeing for three months. I felt she was way too young for that.

"I know that more and more teens are losing their virginity at fifteen. But I worried about how the audience would take it. I still believe there are virgins in this world, girls who want to say no. I really didn't want teens all over the world thinking it was okay."

Shannen lost her battle and the episode was filmed exactly as it was written. It did spark some controversey across America; angry parents wrote in complaining about the show. "We received letters from parents who said they trusted us and we let them down," says Darren Star. "My mother told me it shouldn't have been done. Then I realized this was the first conversation we'd ever had about sex." Charles Rosin says the show might have to cut its plans to examine teen sexuality to the fullest in the future. "I don't think we'll be exploring as many sexual issues because of the climate today," he remarks.

When Shannen spoke her mind again, Rosin listened and did change the script. Because she is a role model to teenage girls everywhere, she was very concerned that the writers always had Brenda dieting. "There was an instance in a script where they kept having Brenda say, 'I've got to lose five pounds,'" says Shannen. "But Im a very thin person. So I sat down with Chuck Rosin and I said, 'Chuck, I'm the thinnest girl on the show! If girls hear Brenda say she can't go to the beach unless she loses weight, they're going to become bulimic! So many young girls already have this problem.' Chuck saw my point immediately. It was out of the script the next day."

There are times Jason is really not sure why they have Brandon fall in and out of love so much. On that subject he says, "Brandon does have a lot of girls, but I think it's pretty true to life. I remember that is one thing that I think everybody goes through in high school. You think you fall in love every week, but you really don't know what love is."

Jason is hoping to play out Brandon's darker side. "Brandon definitely has a bad side, we just haven't seen it yet," he offers. "In the beginning, he was a little too righteous. He's becoming a lot more fallible, a lot more human. We saw a little flash of his other side when he got drunk and crashed his car. I think there's more to come!"

How much more? What will Brandon be up to in the coming year? To those questions, Jason just smiles. "I'm not saying a word," he says slyly. "You're just going to have to tune in next week to find out!"

9
JASON'S ROMANTIC SIDE

Shannen Doherty says if she had to be attracted to any actor on *90210*, it would be her on-screen brother, Jason Priestley. "He is gorgeous," she says. "He has those eyes. I mean, I would *definitely* be attracted to Jason."

The show's producer, Aaron Spelling, comments, "I think Jason is the date that every girl would like to have. He's very attractive, he's sensitive, and he seems safe."

Even though Jason Priestley is extremely

flattered by all this attention, he feels puzzled and downright flustered when girls swoon and scream over him. The truth is, he never thought of himself as the kind of guy who would inspire such passion in the hearts of so many young girls.

But that's just what he's done. And now those millions of admirers want to know the answer to the burning question: what kind of girl does their dream guy go for?

"When it comes to girls, I find things in most every girl that I meet that I like," says Jason, the world's most eligible bachelor. "I don't shut myself off thinking I want someone with blond hair and blue eyes. That's shutting out brunettes, redheads, and all the other wonderful girls out there!"

Even though Jason is not into "getting attached" right now, he gets very serious when it comes to matters of the heart. For example, this romantic guy admits he's a one-woman man. He thinks the worst thing a guy can do is go after someone else's girlfriend. "It's such bad karma," he says, "and somebody will do that to you in return someday."

The kind of girl who turns Jason's head is "someone who has a vibe of openness and niceness. I'm not a playboy," he says. "I like dating one girl at a time—it's a lot more comfortable. I like someone who can communicate with me and who has a good sense of humor. A girl's personality is the most important thing. Aesthetics plays an important part, but it only takes you so far."

Jason also goes for a girl with her own career, who is independent and self-sufficient. His admiration for career-minded women stems from his family background. His mom is proof that a woman doesn't have to give up her career to be a wife and mother. Jason's mom has always been very much her own person and a positive influence in shaping her son's attitude about the opposite sex.

Also, Jason's sister is one of the most independent girls he knows. Justine is a self-proclaimed world traveler who has visited nearly every country on the globe. Now living in London, she's been all over Europe and Asia, and spent a year on safari in Africa.

Jason says he likes a little aggressiveness in girls but adds, smiling, "not too much." He appreciates someone who is natural and who expresses her feelings candidly. He likes a girl who is "beautiful inside and out. Someone very honest and down-to-earth."

When the question of dating came up in a recent interview, Jason revealed, "I like to keep my relationships private. I'm not married, but I have a girlfriend I've been dating for a while."

The girl in question is the pretty actress Robyn Lively. Jason and Robyn met when they costarred in the TV movie *Teen Angel Returns*. In the film, Jason played an angel who comes down from heaven to help Robyn's character out of trouble. While their on-screen chemistry was dynamite, offscreen they realized how much they liked each other. The two quickly became a couple on the set and have dated on and off for two years.

During the filming of *Teen Angel Returns*, Jason and Robyn found out they had a lot in common and would talk about their early years for hours. Robyn was also raised in a show-business environment. Her dad, Ernie Lively, is a respected acting coach; her mom and older brother were both actors. Like Jason, Robyn began her career in television commercials, then moved successfully into film and TV. She's appeared in countless productions, including *Teen Witch*, *The Karate Kid III*, and episodes of *Doogie Howser, M.D.* and *Twin Peaks*. She was even nominated for a Daytime Emmy Award for the *After School Special* "The Less Than Perfect Daughter."

Jason doesn't mind dating someone in the business because he feels actresses understand his job more than anyone else. "If I have to go away on a publicity tour or something, they know it's all part of the work I do," he says.

As far back as junior high school, this sweet guy has always had a way with the ladies. And the reason is because he's always known how to show his girlfriend a good time. He's a spur-of-the-moment kind of guy and likes taking his date to his favorite places at a moment's notice. Jason's idea of a great night out is going to dinner, catching a movie, taking a stroll on the beach, or dancing the night away in a fun hot spot. "My favorite place to hang out and go dancing in L.A. is the Cheesecake Factory," he says with a grin. "They play terrific music and I always have a great time."

Since becoming one of television's most

popular guys, Jason has had to put his romantic life on the back burner. While he is still seeing Robyn, his crazy schedule has definitely cut their time together and cooled their relationship. "Actually, a part of my contract that I didn't see before says I can't have a social life," he offers.

But Jason doesn't seem to be complaining. He knows there is plenty of time for romance and love and marriage, and right now he isn't rushing into anything. His mind-blowing surge of popularity continues to reach explosive proportions and Jason isn't about to let it all slip by him.

"People always say to me, 'Do you think you're missing out on a social life by working so much?' They ask me, 'Are you having fun?' " explains Jason. "I don't have time for much of a social life but I do have some time for dating. And, yes, I am having a lot of fun with the show and the fans. I never expected anything like this to happen to me!"

Underneath the glamorous exterior of being a top teen idol, Jason is just a regular guy looking forward to meeting someone he will want to spend the rest of his life with.

It's still too early to tell who will win Jason's heart. But everyone agrees the person to take this adorable guy out of circulation will be very lucky.

10
THE SECRET OF HIS SUCCESS

There is a crowd of fans gathering outside Torrance High School in Orange County, California, the actual location for 90210's fictitious West Beverly Hills High. They stand outside the closed-off area where their favorite series is being filmed and try to catch a glimpse of the show's star, Jason Priestley.

As the sun begins to set, the group gets smaller, but some fans remain. They've been waiting there for two hours and are determined not to leave until Jason comes out. Finally, their idol emerges.

One girl shrieks, "Hasn't he got the *bluest* eyes?" while another asks for his autograph. Since Jason was pleased with his day's work, he happily obliges, scribbling his name for his fans.

Does he really enjoy this part of his job? Jason nods yes, but seems bemused, even embarrassed, by all the attention. Watching him in action, you immediately form the impression that all this adulation is overpowering.

It's always difficult for newly established stars to cope with the loss of anonymity, and Jason admits that's been the roughest part of achieving success.

Imagine what it would be like to wake up one day and discover that you could no longer walk out your front door. "I like to go shopping once in a while," he says. "But now there's no way I can walk around a mall without being recognized. It's potentially dangerous."

On the contrary, Jason can't walk around *anywhere* without fans rushing up to him—all over the United States as well as in England, where *90210* is the number one show.

The British teens are just as wild about

Jason as the kids in the United States. Because the show is so popular in England, 90210 won an award from Prince Edward, and five cast members (Jason, Shannen, Gabrielle, Ian, and Jennie) were invited to England to receive the award and be given a grand tour of the country.

Jason and the 90210 gang were treated like megastars in England and were excited to be there. From the moment they stepped off the plane, there were screaming fans and photographers following them everywhere they went. The cast had a blast visiting the famous sights, including Buckingham Palace, Trafalgar Square, and the London Zoo. While Jennie, Gabrielle, and Shannen spent time shopping, Jason went to visit his sister, Justine, who lives in London. "My sister can't believe all the stuff going on with my career." He smiles. "She laughs about the amount of fan mail I'm receiving."

Because he has been to see his sister many times, Jason knows his way around London. When nighttime came, he decided to show his cast mates the very best clubs in the area. The happy fivesome hopped from one to another having a grand old time well into the night.

Naturally, the British fans were ecstatic to meet some of the show's stars up close. "I didn't know how popular we were in England," says Jason. "Before we went, I was talking to someone on the phone and he said, 'You don't know what you are in for.' I said, 'Why? We're just going over to do a couple of talk shows and get our award.' And he told me, 'The show is a phenomenon over there. It's number one. Everybody's talking about it.' I have never experienced anything like our trip to England. It was wild."

Gabrielle says, "We were mobbed everywhere we went," while Jennie offers, "The girls were practically climbing over me to get to Jason!"

Even though it may seem understandable for Jason to lose patience with his overly enthusiastic fans, he hasn't reacted like that at all. Instead, he goes out of his way to be kind and considerate to the fans who have propelled him into the superstardom he is enjoying today. "I feel comfortable with it all," he says. "I really don't mind signing autographs. I like being looked up to as a role model. It's all part of being on a show like 90210."

Jason has a heart of gold. He began getting involved with participating in charity events when he was on *Sister Kate*. In November 1990 he was one of the celebs who turned out at the Los Angeles Zoo to help kick off Mattel Toys' national charity event to benefit needy children. Mattel donated $2 million in new toys and gave $250,000 in cash to promote Mattel Kids Care, Too, a campaign that encouraged kids to donate one of their favorite toys to a child less fortunate. At the event, Jason, who went with four of his cast mates from *Sister Kate*, told one reporter, "I'll go to any event that will help a kid in need."

His feelings have never changed. He still feels strongly about donating his time to some charity events. "The best part of being in the public eye is having the opportunity to be able to get out and spend time with kids who are sick or in trouble," he says. "I've met abused kids and done charity work to help children with AIDS. To be able to go out and touch these kids' lives and make them laugh is the best feeling. You know, some of the kids I've met are completely shut off. They have no emotional register at all. It's important to me to be able to bring a smile to the face of a kid who hasn't smiled in a long time."

In June 1991, Jason and his *90210* costars Luke Perry and Brian Austin Green played softball in a celebrity game for the T. J. Martell Foundation. Dressed in shorts and a T-shirt with the words "Rebel Guy" printed across the chest, Jason looked great out on the University of Southern California field. He was happy to hear his team helped raise $400,000 for children with cancer, AIDS, and leukemia, but slightly disappointed that they lost the game by one run. With a grin, he said, "We can't let that get us down, because everything else went so good today."

One very serious subject Jason speaks out on is teenage drinking and driving. His own teenage years did not go by without the question of drugs and alcohol coming up. He does proudly admit that he has never touched drugs at all and if he did have an occasional drink, he surely didn't drive. He went through a very difficult time in high school when two of his friends died in drunk-driving accidents. He also remembers a wild party he attended when he was sixteen where a girl who had been drinking very heavily tried to commit suicide. Those incidents haunt him to this day. Because he saw how drinking could destroy someone's life, it helped him survive his own difficult teen years.

Jason credits his dad for helping him out with anything that was bothering him while he was growing up. "I have a great relationship with my father," says Jason. "Whenever I had any problems I took them to him. I always respected his judgment."

Jason's father was always understanding and straightforward with his son. On the subject of drinking, for example, Lorne told Jason, "I know you may have a drink once in a while at a party and that's fine. But whatever you do, don't get in the car. Call me and I'll come and I'll pick you up."

Today, as a teen role model, these are Jason's views on teenage drinking: "When you're young, you think you drink alcohol to have a good time. But if you're confused and insecure and things are happening to you that you don't understand, drinking and those basic teenager insecurities can be a lethal combination."

Jason believes kids face a great deal and must make decisions carefully. "Teenagers nowadays have so many more pressures," he says. "There are many more things that teens are exposed to as opposed to what went on in the fifties and sixties. It definitely forces you to grow up in a hurry."

Jason's concern for the subject of drinking and driving inspired him and a friend to film their own short movie called *One Single Raindrop*. Jason wrote, produced, directed, and starred in the film, which dealt with drunk driving. Told in flashbacks, the story centers on two friends and explores how one deals with the death of the other after he is killed by a drunk driver. There are no plans to release the film right now. Jason was happy the subject of drinking and driving was tackled on an episode of *90210*.

11

"THIS IS WHO I REALLY AM!"

"Brandon is such a nice guy," Jason says. "Far nicer than me." It seems that Jason is doing his best to make sure he's different in every way from Brandon Walsh. But is he *really*? He plays him so believably every week, there must be a part of his own personality in there somewhere.

Recently, Jason compared himself to his character by saying, "I've experienced a lot more than Brandon. I'm not naive. There *is* a part of me that's like Brandon, though— he has all that youthful energy and exuberance."

As Jason continues to win hearts all over the country, fans want to know what he's *really* like. Girls everywhere appreciate his innate sensitivity and love his terrific looks. He has a nation of *90210* fans responding to his honesty, forthrightness, and idealism.

Has success spoiled Jason?

Superstardom is something most people want until they actually have it. Jason has achieved a level of superstardom, but he finds it difficult to think of himself as a celebrity. His overnight success has left him remarkably unaffected.

Jason always strives for perfection in his career, and he works so hard at his craft that he makes a conscious effort to keep his life away from the cameras a very private one. When he has a free day, he's content with spending time with close friends or just relaxing in his brand new condo.

Jason's greatest asset is his integrity, and pretentious Hollywood glitz doesn't particularly interest him. He has stubbornly refused to become part of the Hollywood social swirl or to join other actors in the endless round of parties.

Jason would much rather hop on his Yamaha motorcycle or get in his Alfa Romeo and tool around, seeing parts of California he's never seen before. He loves the feeling of speeding through the countryside, finding roads rarely traveled.

To escape the stress and pressure of show business, Jason goes to the ocean; he loves the wide-open feeling it inspires. One of his passions is sailing, and when he has some time to himself, you can often spot him at the marina. "I'm saving up to buy my own sailboat," he says. "My dad owns a boat, and every year we participate in the winter racing series in Vancouver. But last year I couldn't get back home because I was working, and I really missed it."

Jason has learned that there is a price attached to achieving fame. Besides becoming a superstar and sex symbol, he also became a target for criticism. One frequent accusation is that success has turned Jason's head and made him temperamental, arrogant, and difficult to work with. But the report from the 90210 set is just the opposite. The cast and crew praise Jason for his professionalism and sense of humor.

Brian Green says, "Jason is never negative about anything. He's a real positive influence, honest, caring, and respectful." Luke

Perry reveals, "Jay is a lot of fun on the outside and very professional on the inside." Shannen Doherty says of her on-screen twin brother, "Jason has a wild side. He's always playing pranks on the set." Pondering his personality even further, she quickly adds, "I don't think he likes anyone to see his vulnerability."

"Many people don't realize that being an actor takes a lot of discipline and commitment. Our whole crew on the show works as hard as the actors, and I never want to sell myself short. I want to get in there and contribute as much as I can," asserts Jason.

Still the rumors continue. There are people who claim that now that he has become a celebrity, he has no desire to associate with his former friends. "Man, who starts those rumors?" is Jason's reaction. "I still talk to the guys I went to high school with."

He feels the story may have started because of the chunk of time his hectic work schedule takes from his personal life. "I'm out of bed most mornings before the sun comes up and I don't get home until way after dark," he confides. "So when my friends knock on my door and ask me to go out, I have to tell them no. Otherwise my tiredness will show up in my performance the next day."

Others say that the negative rumors about Jason are false. In fact, he prefers not to receive the star treatment. "I like it when people act like themselves around me, act normal," he says. "Since all this started, it's something I don't get very much of anymore."

Jason Priestley just enjoys a day away from the spotlight. He loves to stay home, wear comfy clothes like jeans and a T-shirt, and listen to music by Elvis Costello or Fine Young Cannibals. He owns a large collection of videos and loves watching his favorite movies, *A Clockwork Orange* and *Blue Velvet*. He doesn't like to shave every day and often sports some stubble on his gorgeous face. When he doesn't have to work, he pops out his contact lenses and puts on his round, horn-rimmed glasses. His only vice is smoking cigarettes. Jason is an individual who is unpredictable and unconventional.

Jason is a stickler about keeping his living space extremely tidy. Not long after striking gold with 90210, he moved his belongings into a new condo, a big step from his previous place. When he arrived in California from Canada, his first apartment was modest.

Jason grew up in a very clean, neat, and comfortable home. His mom had trained him to pick up his clothes and keep his own room presentable. Neatness became a habit, and even if his first apartment was cheap, you can bet he always had everything in its proper order.

"I'm a neatness freak!" admits Jason. "I think it has something to do with the fact that I was born under the astrological sign of Virgo, because Virgos tend to be very organized and clean."

Jason set up a home office in one room of his condo. His big walnut desk is situated right next to a window. In back of his desk, there is a wall of shelves that Jason set up neatly with books, framed photographs, his video collection, and some special mementos. His phone and answering machine are to the right on his desk, a cup of pencils and pens are on the first shelf of the middle bookcase at arm's reach, and his script for the day rests on a second shelf. With everything in its proper place, Jason has whatever he needs at his fingertips at all times.

Given his orderliness, it's rare that any of Jason's possessions are ever misplaced, though sometimes things do get shifted around. "When that happens, I get so angry," he says. "It drives me crazy if I can't find something when I need it."

Restless by nature, Jason constantly tries to find things to fill every hour of every day. "When I have time off, I hate it when I have nothing to do," he says. "That's why I'm forever taking up a new hobby."

One hobby he took up years ago is cooking. When he was growing up, Jason loved to whip up meals for his family. Spending time in the kitchen refining his culinary skills, he has become an excellent cook.

"I love cooking!" says Jason, whose specialties include Mexican and Chinese dishes. "Mexican food is my favorite," he exclaims. "I can cook Mexican food like a maniac."

In his spare time, Jason enjoys playing basketball, and he devotes Sundays to playing center on a division-two hockey team that competes against NHL veterans. Recently, he's taken up golf and spends a great deal of time perfecting his game. Other favorite sports include tennis, snow skiing, and his latest love—bungee jumping. The only problem he faces is finding time to do the things he enjoys. His long days on the set leave him too tired. "Most of the time I just want to go home and go to sleep," he admits.

Jason Priestley has come a long way from the boy who began acting in commercials in Canada to becoming the hottest teen star on television's hottest show.

There's no denying the fact that Jason is a star in every sense of the word, and when he does get the time and ambition to try a new endeavor, he has the opportunity to do so. His success has enabled him to make all his dreams come true.

12
NEW DIRECTIONS

Jason may be a superstar, but he still has goals he would like to attain in the coming years. Even though he's hit the big time with *90210*, he's always looking for ways to expand and improve himself as an actor—and he's always checking out new areas he'd like to develop.

One such area is working behind the scenes, especially behind the camera. On more than one occasion, Jason has expressed interest in directing, but admits he will achieve that goal "years from now. I must first master one craft before moving on to the next."

Beverly Hills, 90210 remains the jewel in Jason's crown of stardom and he isn't about to turn his back on it now. "I'll play Brandon as long as they need and want me," he insists. "I only worry that they can't keep us in high school much longer."

That thought has also crossed the mind of Darren Star. Even though the Walsh twins are seniors at West Beverly Hills High School, Star says there's no rush to have them graduate. "Their senior year may go on for two more seasons," he predicts. "But they won't be in high school forever."

Everyone involved with *90210* is as determined as Jason Priestley is to keep getting better, to reach a larger audience, and to continue exploring new themes. Even though Jason doesn't like to comment on the show's future, executive producer Charles Rosin shares his feelings when he says, "We're trying to look at what's happening in contemporary society, how that affects teenagers, and how we can explore those things through our characters. You could do a show called *Beverly Hills, 90210* and fill it full of stereotypes. But we're not doing that. Even with scenes at a beach club, it's not *Beach Blanket Bingo*. We're making a concerted effort to keep the show unpredictable. We'll have some light-hearted episodes, we'll use music, we'll make it more eclectic. We're opting for substance, not style."

Jason feels exactly the same way. In the future, he wants to continue to do quality work, even if it means not doing it in great quantity.

Besides the security of success, Jason is now enjoying financial security as well. He's become a hot property in Hollywood and it's already being predicted that he will make the transition from the small screen to the silver screen. Following in the footsteps of successful actors like Michael J. Fox, Richard Grieco, and Johnny Depp, no doubt Jason will leave his impact on film the way he did on TV. Jason possesses a lot of fire, and he produces deep emotions. The insiders in show business are behind him 100 percent.

But Jason is not entirely ready to be wined and dined by the big bosses at the major studios. "Everything's going way too fast. I just want to take one step at a time," he says.

Jason has already proven what he could do by getting the green light from a producer. He was a relative newcomer when they put him in the driver's seat of 90210, and he helped to drive it straight into the hearts of millions. He's the kind of actor movie producers like to invest in. As for his own future, Jason is clearly in the driver's seat and he's traveling at rocketlike speed, heading for more exciting projects.

Jason often discusses his future with Ian Ziering and Luke Perry on the set of 90210. Jason and Ian both have an eye on writing and have worked together on ideas for future episodes. So far, they are still working on the scripts, and have not submitted them yet.

It isn't unusual for Jason and his two costars to talk seriously about the years ahead. "We often talk about going into business together," says Jason. "We've talked about pooling our resources and opening up a restaurant. I think we all know what an uncertain business acting can be, and it's comforting to think of doing something else if it all fell apart tomorrow."

Jason should know by now that there's no danger of his acting career ending today—

or tomorrow—or anytime in the future. He's simply too much in demand; he's hot, and his sizzling career is only getting hotter. Jason has polished his talents from his raw early years, but he hasn't lost his ambition and drive. To remain on top, he knows that he must continue to extend himself beyond his boundaries.

He has already mapped out a long list of things to accomplish in the future. He wants more of the same, only bigger and better, and there's no reason why today's top teen idol can't become one of tomorrow's top stars. Professionally, he can be anything he wants to be: actor on stage and screen, director, writer, even restaurant owner.

Jason possesses the quality of a confident, easygoing guy—and he will consistently come out on top. He knows what he wants and he has the determination, drive, and brash charm to continue to get it. But Jason is realistic: he knows he must take one day at a time and continue to work. As he continues to do that, his career will keep rolling along at the same exciting pace for many years to come. Jason Priestley is here to stay!

JASON'S CHECKLIST FACT FILE

FULL NAME: Jason Bradford Priestley

BIRTHDATE: August 28, 1969

BIRTHPLACE: Vancouver, British Columbia, Canada

HAIR COLOR: Light brown

EYE COLOR: Blue-green-gray

HEIGHT: 5'9"

WEIGHT: 140 lbs.

FAMILY: Jason's mom, Sharon, used to be an actress/choreographer/ballerina. She is now a real estate agent. His dad, Lorne, is a manufacturer's representative for a furniture and textile company. His sister, Justine, is eighteen months older than Jason. She is a world traveler who has been on safari in Africa and now lives in England.

FAVORITE MOTORCYCLE: Yamaha

FAVORITE CAR: Alfa Romeo

FAVORITE SINGERS: Elvis Costello, Paula Abdul

FAVORITE GROUP: Fine Young Cannibals

FAVORITE FOODS: Mexican, Chinese

FAVORITE ACTORS: Robert Duvall, Al Pacino, John Savage

FAVORITE MOVIES: *A Clockwork Orange*, *Blue Velvet*

FAVOTIRE TV SHOWS: *CNN News*, *Married . . . With Children*

FAVORITE COLOR: Blue

FAVORITE SPORTS: Hockey, rugby, sailing, golf, basketball

FAVORITE HOBBY: Going bungee jumping with Luke Perry

OTHER AMBITIONS: During high school, he wanted to play professional hockey, but he wasn't tall enough

FIRST ROLE: Canadian TV movie *Stacey* at age eight

TV MOVIES: *Lies from Lotus Land*, *Nobody's Child*, and for the Disney channel *Teen Angel* and *Teen Angel Returns*

TV ROLES: Guest starred in *21 Jump Street*,

MacGyver, The Adventures of Beans Baxter, Airwolf II, Danger Bay, Quantum Leap. Played series regular Todd Mahaffey on short-lived TV show *Sister Kate*. Now playing Brandon Walsh on *Beverly Hills, 90210*

FILM APPEARANCES: *Watchers, The Boy Who Could Fly, Nowhere to Run, Caddo Lake*

JUICY JASON SECRETS

Jason says he'll try any sport "as long as it's dangerous and life-threatening."

◆

Like his buddy Luke Perry's, Jason's pet is also a black pot-bellied pig. Jason named his porky friend Dave, while Luke's is called Jerry Lee.

◆

Jason's nickname for costar Shannen Doherty is "Shannendoah."

◆

Working with kids on *Sister Kate* made him appreciate them more. "I love kids," he says. "The kids on *Sister Kate* looked up to me and treated me like their role model. They saw me like some kind of funky old man."

◆

Jason has become close pals with Tommy Puett, the musician-actor who plays Tyler Benchfield on TV's *Life Goes On*. He says, "We have a lot in common. We're both serious about acting *and* music."

◆

Jason plays the drums and spends a lot of time on the set of *90210* practicing with fellow cast mate Brian Green, whose dad is a professional drummer.

◆

Jason is a practical joker and loves doing impressions of show-business personalities. He does a great impression of the comedian Andrew Dice Clay.

His closest friends and family call him Jay.

◆

His fantasy is to buy a sailboat, take off one year, and sail around the world.

◆

Jason would like to have a falcon or a hawk as a pet bcause he thinks they are beautiful, exotic birds. "It's so cool, you get to wear those little gloves and put that little helmet on them so they can't see," he says.

◆

Jason has been compared to actor Michael J. Fox but claims, "I think it's just because we're both from Canada."

◆

Jason won the role of Todd on *Sister Kate* after only two auditions—usually it takes eight or nine to land a role.

HEY, JAY, WHAT DO YOU SAY?

On Himself

"Even though I like to do some wild and exciting things, I'm just a regular fun-loving guy."

On Acting

"You can never be perfect when it comes to acting. There's always more to learn."

"I'm never nervous when I'm working. I get more nervous being myself."

On His Real-Life High School vs. West Beverly Hills High

"My high school and this high school are drastically different, but the experiences don't change."

On Values

"I suppose when you reach adulthood, you pretty much have your values and morals set. Speaking as an adult, I can honestly say I do have a lot of values."

On Girls

"I like all kinds of different girls. I go for variety, you know? It's kind of like you get these little cereal variety packs. You can have Fruit Loops, or Sugar Smacks, or Product 19. To me, it's the same with girls. I like blondes, brunettes, redheads. I love 'em all!"

On His Most Prized Possession

"I love cars. Cars are my passion. Right now, I have an Italian sports car, an Alfa Romeo."

On His Beverly Hills, 90210 *Costars*

"We all do fun things together. One time, there were six birthdays on the set. We were trying to rehearse, but all these cakes kept showing up and there were presents everywhere. I really like being part of this show."

On Visiting Canada

"I miss Vancouver. It's an amazing city, it's so beautiful and clean. I love it. I go back home whenever I can to go skiing and to visit my family. I still have some close friends I keep in touch with."

On His Future

"I just can't see myself sitting behind a desk all day, so I think I will always do something creative. Hopefully, if acting didn't work out for me, I could get into something else in entertainment like directing or writing. I just love this business too much to even think of doing anything else."

ABOUT THE AUTHOR

GRACE CATALANO is the author of two *New York Times* best-sellers: *New Kids on the Block* and *New Kids on the Block Scrapbook*. Her other books include biographies of Paula Abdul, Gloria Estefan, Richard Grieco, Fred Savage, River Phoenix, Alyssa Milano, and Kirk Cameron. She is also the author of *Teen Star Yearbook*, which includes minibiographies of eighty-five celebrities. Grace is currently the editor of the teen magazines *Dream Guys* and *Dream Guys Presents*. She and her brother, Joseph, wrote and designed *Elvis: A Tenth Anniversary Tribute* and *Elvis and Priscilla*. Grace lives on the North Shore of Long Island.